THE BEST
NEW BRITISH
AND IRISH
POETS
2016

JUDGED AND EDITED BY
KELLY DAVIO
SERIES EDITOR
TODD SWIFT

THE BEST NEW BRITISH AND IRISH POETS 2016

EYEWEAR PUBLISHING

First published in 2016
by Eyewear Publishing Ltd
Suite 333, 19-21 Crawford Street
Marylebone, London W1H 1PJ
United Kingdom

Cover design and typeset by Edwin Smet
Printed in England by TJ International Ltd, Padstow, Cornwall

ISBN 978-1-908998-55-2

Eyewear wishes to thank Jonathan Wonham
for his generous patronage of our press.

WWW.EYEWEARPUBLISHING.COM

This book
is dedicated to
the poet

RODDY LUMSDEN

who has done so much over the
years to encourage the
new poets of Britain
and Ireland.

Table of Contents

INTRODUCTION

Welcome to *The Best New British and Irish Poets 2016*, Eyewear Publishing's inaugural anthology of fifty poems from emerging writers in these isles. This new series takes as its model the long-standing American series, *Best New Poets* – published by the University of Virginia Press – which has become an important feature of the greater literary landscape of the United States.

Like the American series, *The Best New British and Irish Poets* seeks to introduce to the reading public poets whose work we feel should be part of a wider conversation about poetry. We anticipate that the poets in these pages, rising stars as they are, will all go on to publish widely in the future, but we also believe that these fifty poets and their work are exciting, galvanising, and relevant *now*, in the early stages of their careers.

But just what do we mean by 'emerging poet', anyway? 'Emerging poet' is a slippery term (and one that sounds, let's face it, unfortunately primordial), but in the case of this anthology, we mean simply a poet who had not yet come under contract to publish their debut full-length poetry collection at the time of their submission. Any poet resident in, or a citizen of, either the UK or Ireland who met that description at the time of our reading period was eligible to nominate him or herself for inclusion among the final fifty poets in this anthology – no academic nominations, no arm-twisting by influential journals, but simply a democratic process by which any qualifying poet writing in the English language could put work forward for consideration. As an American writer recently transplanted to England, that kind of process — one that values an equal chance for any writer, regardless of age, publication record, or hometown — appeals to my sense of fair play and opportunity.

And as a new kid on the block, I was particularly excited when Todd Swift, series editor for *The Best New British and Irish Poets*, approached me about judging this year's group of entries. I myself benefited greatly from inclusion in the American series, and recognition in *Best New Poets* was an honour that I coveted more than I'd like to admit (and I'll go so far as to confess that when I received news that I was among the final 50 for the 2009 anthology, I let out a barbaric yawp — to borrow from my countryman Walt Whitman — that no doubt startled the neighbors). I believed then that being among the 'best' would open doors in my writing career that I hadn't even had the courage to rap lightly on before.

It's true that new opportunities came to me as a poet in the months after the anthology came out, but much more important were the relationships I'd go on to forge with many of the other poets in the volume; I discovered writers whose work challenged me as a reader, and whom I got to know as engaged members of the larger literary ecosystem. As our writing careers have moved forward, many of us have remained in touch, and have formed a supportive literary community. It's my hope that the writers represented in these pages will have the same experience, and that artistic alliances and personal friendships will develop from this collection of poets and will stand as nurturing influences in the years to come.

But beyond my having a personal connection with the American series, *what's an American editor doing judging British and Irish writing?*, you may be wondering. What could I possibly know about the landscape of contemporary poetry some 4,700 miles from my home?

Those are fair enough questions, and in response I'll offer the following: we American poets know there is a great deal we can appreciate in our transatlantic counterparts. Some of our great English-language American poets, like Sylvia Plath and T.S. Eliot, to name just two, did some of their greatest work while here in England, steeped in the forms, rhythms, and traditions of our common tongue. And British-born poets who moved to or even simply spent time in America – Anne Bradstreet, Denise Levertov, and W. H. Auden, again to select just a small handful – contributed work that's become foundational to the American literary landscape. All of these poets hold in common an immense respect for the craft of the poem itself: an attention to the unit of the line, to the musicality of the language, and to the memory of the forms that have been observed, adapted, and reinvented so fruitfully over time. It's my hope that this anthology will be read both here in England, Scotland, Wales, and Ireland, as well as in the United States, and that the literary conversation between our cultures can benefit from seeing that tradition of careful craftsmanship at work here in these pages.

It's also the case that, as an editor who's spent the better part of the last decade helming literary journals in America, I've gotten quite familiar with the names, the personalities, and the politics in my own poetry communities. It's awfully hard for an editor deeply familiar with submitters' work to curate any selection without dragging a certain amount of baggage along in the process. But in editing this anthology, reading submissions from poets who were all more or less new to me was a welcome opportunity to appreciate, to enjoy, to be dazzled by poetic talent without any preconceived notions or expectations. For the poets included here, I hope that my fresh eyes on their poems may stand as a validating force: I selected their work based on its strength and its strength alone.

And just what were the strengths I was looking for in vetting the submissions for this anthology? One of the most important recent shifts in the poetry of my home country is a shift I'm eager to watch here in England: a shift toward a poetry of social engagement. Young American poets – if I may paint with very broad strokes – have become less interested in highly personal work and more interested in grappling with the most difficult issues that face our country: racism, religious intolerance, misogyny, police brutality, homophobia, and environmental destruction, to name a few. I was looking, in these poems, for the kind of social consciousness that can bravely allow a poem to be political. I found it there in Alan Dunnett's quietly poignant 'Succour', in Tiffany Anne Tondut's historical but relevant 'Canary Girls', and in Maria Isakova-Bennett's heartbreaking 'Adrift'.

I was looking, too, for poetry that placed itself in conversation with that of the poets who've gone before us, which I found in Victoria Kennefick's poem of pilgrimage 'Visiting Sylvia', and in Colin Dardis' work with received form in 'Easter Tuesday, 1941'. I was looking for poems that worked with invented forms as well, as does Holly Corfield Carr's sectioned prose poem 'Loxodrome', and for poems that explore the various possibilities of the line in free verse, as does James Nixon's lively 'It's 11.26 in SE13'. I looked for poems that delighted me with their humour, as did Niall Bourke's 'Unexpected Item In The Bagging Area', and for poems that captivated me with their unexpected imagery the way that Alex Bell's 'Georgia On My Mind' did.

Finally, I waited to be surprised by those poems I didn't see coming – poems like Isabel Rogers' 'The Apiarist' and Tess Jolly's 'Goldfields' – and which were so gorgeously made that they caused this editor pause in gratitude for having been able to experience them.

It's my hope that, as you enter these pages, you'll come to feel as I do about reading these poets: that we're in a privileged position to watch this early stage of their careers, and that we'll be reading their work for years to come. I also hope that, as this anthology series continues year on year, we'll discover even more promising new talent as we celebrate the great tradition of poetry in English.

Kelly Davio
London, UK
March 2016

ALAN DUNNETT

is a former regional theatre director,
whose productions included *Entertaining
Mr Sloane* with Gary Oldman (Chesterfield
Pomegranate) and the large-scale community
play *Bridge* (Dundee Rep). He now works largely
for MA Screen at Drama Centre, Central Saint
Martins, London. Poems have appeared in
magazines and ezines including *Stand*, *The Rialto*,
Poetry News, *Dream Catcher*, *Poetry Salzburg
Review*, *Brittle Star*, *Militant Thistles*, *London
Grip*, *Dead Ink* and *nthposition*. He has won
prizes in competitions including Ealing,
Norwich, Nottingham, Torbay,
Stroud and Kent & Sussex.

Succour

We have nowhere to live.

                I sympathise —

I can't get on the housing list.

                No food —

we have nothing to eat.

                I'm hungry too —

and my kids have it rough.

                We would have died —

we had to get out.

                I sympathise, mate —

but we've got problems here.

                My brother died —

I have his children with me...

                I've got kids —

I blame the eurozone...

                and his young wife —

old before her time.

                  Heating bills are pants —

this isn't paradise.

                  I feel your pain —

God be with you.

                  Try good old Germany —

they owe us one.

                  Thank you. Thanks. May we just

step inside and use your toilet?

                  The flush —

it's busted. Try number ten. Top, top bell.

ALEX BELL

grew up in Northumberland
and Dorset, and lives and works in London.
Her work has appeared in *Magma, The Rialto,
Poetry Wales, A Tower Miscellany* (Tower Poetry,
2010), and *Homesickness and Exile* (The Emma
Press, 2014). She is co-organiser of a series of
poetry and karaoke nights named 'Aoke'
at the Betsey Trotwood in Farringdon.
Bell was longlisted for the National
Poetry Competition 2015.

Georgia On My Mind

When Georgia turns from us, her back is a Man Ray.
We hate to see her go. We love to watch her leave.
With Georgia gone, our hair
is both lank and flyaway. We are hungry.
Our buckles rust, and moths eat at our tweed.
We hold huge boomboxes
over our heads for Georgia. We try to dance her back.
We turn ourselves over like rainsticks,
and the falling organs clatter, and sound like rain,
which we feel must be appealing to Georgia,
who is by turns heavy and light,
and collects in sad pools on impermeable surfaces.
We fear that she is gone away forever.
Sometimes in the Georgialess night
we stitch ourselves together — little floral octagons
in the great thick quilt of our aching for Georgia.
We need her. We need her breadth and the smell of her neck,
and all of snake-spined roads leading back to her.
When in the mornings we wake without Georgia,
the shock pops our monocles. She's meant to be here,
where her skin drifts in motes, and she's bigger
the longer she's gone, as big and as clear
as the moonlight sliding its knife through the pines.

ALEX HOUEN

is author of the poetry
chapbook *Rouge States* (Oystercatcher, 2014)
and has published poems in numerous journals
including *PN Review*, *The Wolf*, *The Fortnightly
Review*, *Visual Verse*, *Molly Bloom*, *Shearsman
Magazine*, and *Free Verse*. His book *Powers of
Possibility: Experimental American Literature since
the 1960s* was published in paperback by
OUP in 2014. He co-edits the online
poetry magazine *Blackbox Manifold*,
and teaches modern literature
at Cambridge.

Goatscape Monologue

When a society breaks down, time sequences shorten
by barter, insult, revenge, or neurotic symptom —
as when a man offers from his richest hand
a plastic bowl foaming with dew of daughter-
in-law, laughing, 'What law? What daughter?'
         From where the partition walls have been
demolished issues a sweet smell of neglected infants
and the floury smell of pubescent boys' beds.
Foreign aliens imitate these beds for having none,
then day and night become confused, sun
comes too close to earth, and life turns
unbearable. Me, I tilled the choice garden of Grace
with its splendid trees and party of statues.
The tall neighbouring structures are collapsing
oversight. That exposed wall —
I broke into a sweat then a run when I felt it
at home in me. It conjures disaster as a date palm
conjures dates. For beyond the city wall it's not clear
that the roaming goats are goats.
Even the smallest goat may be a disastrous blend
of man and dog. I wouldn't know how
to broadcast their number for our dear children
of the cloud. Even without coupling,
the dogs found their folk like a 'big thing',
a second head staring from behind your face,
your heart after you, beating its pulp.
They make room only for a single cause
to absorb all causality in their vision, everything
seen *as if*.
         As if; that was what I called it
when they stood around my bed, took my pulse,
crowned me with parsley to make sweet sport

of fears in a serving of time. Fear that if you fall
asleep some number will grow in your brain until
there is no space for you inside it fear that you lie
on a glass shelf of fear that you'll knock your bowl
from absent-mindedness or loneliness onto the glass
and break into screams and so fearful betray yourself
and speak those fears...

Their mixture of cruelty and credulity
has assumed the proportion of myth.
Under the feet of their leader the earth never grows
again; he need only be himself
to establish his enmity's third remove.
These days I see the very real power the right costume
can exert. I grow more and more daring:
pleated Persian trousers, sweeping cloaks, wraps, shawls,
veils, diadems with stupid expressionless stones,
even a carnival mask that reminds me of a dog we had
who behaved as though he wore one.

Camouflage is an unstable memory that pools
into the deadpan. Since envy and solidarity are better
than pity, I have offered up fireless offerings to our
cumulus children again. And they have come back to me,
as heavy a burden as ever, and so our bonds of revenge
mature, and I see they have borne us
no reason at all to wonder.

ALI LEWIS

is a 25-year-old poet.
His work has been published in *Magma*,
Brittle Star and online, and in anthologies from
The Emma Press and Live Canon. He was highly
commended in the PBS National Student Poetry
Competition, and a runner-up in the Poetry
Book Fair Competition 2015. He has a degree
in politics from Cambridge University,
and is studying for an MA in Creative
Writing at Goldsmiths College.
He works for The
Poetry School.

Ab(so)lution

Simply by gathering
in a pool in my hands
the cut-crystal rope it
extrudes from its faucet;
by rebaptising my face
in its font-waters,
post-urination, I,
kneeling the while on stone
in orthodox prayer,
have transmuted, by
miracle, bathtub to basin,
and in doing so have
made myself smaller,
more young, and therefore
more brave, as I do
the not-so-brave
things I already do,
and forgivable, having
done unforgivable things.

AMY McCAULEY

has had poetry, essays and reviews appear
widely in magazines and anthologies including
The Poetry of Sex (Viking), *Hallelujah for
50ft Women* (Bloodaxe), *Best British Poetry 2015*
(Salt), *Poetry Wales*, *The Quietus* and *The Rialto*.
Her pamphlet *Slops* was shortlisted for
the Pighog/Poetry School Prize 2014 and in
2008 she was shortlisted for the Bridport
Prize. Her current projects include a
collection of poems (*Auto-Oedipa*)
which re-imagines the
Oedipus myth.

Ithakafor

You say I'm a fool to hold the
future by the

throat but / darling / I can't help wondering
what these Ithakas

mean & now I'm the wrong side of thirty all that bedsit slap
& tickle just

seems *sooooo* last century / so I take my pills every day like a good girl
& keep my

crushes to myself & I'll be damned if I don't make it to the end in/tact whatever the
poxy oracles say /

so no more drinking the bar dry / no more illicit chemical kicks & no more round-the-
clock- karaoke-lock-ins / O

cuz *girls just wanna have fun*'s a lie if fun means nothing left to lose / besides / I'm a
sucker for Schubert

& all that syphilitic jazz / I'm a sucker for the endlessly quotable sea & these
little Ithakas / maybe

I'll never know what they mean & maybe that's for the best & baby
you're right / I

should kick my heels for a bit / let everything slide in this
strange unliveable place /

only answer me this: what can I do but feed
the beast my

ugly words & get no applause
?

~

ANDREW FENTHAM

is a poet and translator
from Birmingham. His work has
appeared in magazines and anthologies in the
UK, Ireland, France and Hungary. *Project*
appeared as an installation at the Hatton Gallery
(Newcastle upon Tyne) in 2015. He was awarded
a New Poet Bursary by New Writing North in
2013 and recently completed an MA Creative
Writing at Newcastle University where he
was awarded the Taught Masters Prize
for Creative Writing. He lives and
works in Cornwall.

I Can Has Snowclone?

What have you been gathering today, little sister?
My snake is a diabolical signature; my cat
has a Pop Tart for a body. The snake will eat
its tail; a sea squirt wears a tunic and eats

its own brain. Meme is the new snowclone.
Cloud of knowing, *anima mundi*, grant me
∞∞∞∞∞∞∞∞∞ **INFINITE LIVES** ∞∞∞∞∞∞∞∞∞
that I may copy and paste myself into Lethe.

ANNABEL BANKS

won both of Cambridge University's writing prizes (the Ryan Kinsella Poetry Prize and the RSC 'Other' Prize for theatre), then won full funding for both her prose MA and poetry PhD. In 2015 her work received three nominations for the Pushcart Prize, with further nominations for the Queen's Ferry Press *Best Short Fictions 2016*, Blazevox's *Bettering American Poetry* and the 2016 Derringer Awards. Her work can be found in literary journals, magazines and anthologies including *Envoi*, *The Manchester Review*, *International Times*, *Under the Radar* and *3:AM*. She has also completed her first novel, *The Lockpicker's Guide*, and is working on her second, *I Can Help You Live*.

Ideal State

Plato is telling me to stop, for my sake. He bites
the lead from pencils, pours ink meant for pens
down sneaky rubber hoses sewn into his robe

removes feathers from pillows and the trim
of inherited hats. Every surface must be bleached
back to pale beginnings; even my skin is checked,

(inner-thighs and armpits, the fat pad of my tongue)
in case of contamination. Plato loves me enough
to shave my head, he says. The same old story,

an irritated man home from the pub,
fist-to-wall emphases, tears pink and stinging from
strip-light stares – he hates to blink

as much he hates looking – then it begins:
pages cooked in gravy, flushed down the loo
or hidden in the dishwasher, to be rinsed of words

and pulped back to innocence. He checks my drawers.
Grabs my hand and squeezes, hard. 'I'm doing this for you.'
He really isn't. When it's quiet, I un-strap his sandals,

make tea in playful mugs, and don't let him see
her scratches, or how her bloody feet
kick against my pupils to be free.

BECKY CHERRIMAN

is a writer, workshop leader
and performer based in Leeds.
Published by *Mslexia*, *New Walk*, *Envoi*,
Mother's Milk, *Well Versed* and *Bloodaxe*, she
was resident poet for Morley Literature
Festival in 2013. Her work has appeared on
umbrellas and in the e-book *Poets For Corbyn*.
A current collaboration is *Haunt*, an Imove
commission. Her first pamphlet was recently
released with Mother's Milk Books and her
first full collection will be published by
Cinnamon Press in late 2016.

Urbanite

All they wanted was the drawing in and out of breath.

It didn't matter if it was the laughter of children,
a business woman blowing on a *Cup a Soup*
or couples – their groans toppling
over one another in an avalanche.

They were even grateful for the smack users
who pressed their backs against the walls
and slipped to the underlay,
their sighs blue pilot lights.

And when the yellowjackets came,
breathing nicotine and tenorous commands,
the houses fell gracefully
to gypsum and urbanite, joist and lintel,
bequeathed their treasures to the rubble-raider,
the bone grubber who fingered rusted spoons,
picked apart circuit breakers
and the exposed arteries of an oven.

Loading his spoils on the cart,
he sang and, in a tambour of hooves,
his horse turned and exhaled,
resuscitated I-beam and jamb.

BEN ASHWELL

is a journalist, writer and poet
whose work has appeared in a range of
publications online and in print, including *The
Los Angeles Review of Books, Bookslut, Cake
Literary Magazine* and *The Laura Hird
Showcase*. Originally from Cambridgeshire,
he currently lives and works
in New York.

On Poetry

Everyone wanted to get up on her —
it was the way she puckered those alluring lips.
Long nights spent playing with ourselves and new verse.

Skirt up her thigh, high enough to conjure
hot nights of obsession we couldn't miss.
Everyone wanted to get up on her.

Our thoughts got loose with so many rumours,
what she could do with those raspberry lips.
Long nights spent playing with ourselves and new verse.

Sucking swollen tongues from reciting words
trying to find at least one line that hits.
All we could think of was how to charm her.

The cannons of war were dwarfed next to hers,
falling in love with her myth, rhyme and wit.
Long nights spent playing with ourselves and new verse.

Some nights the words stuck, some nights the words hurt,
some nights we'd lose it thinking of those lips.
We all tried our best to get up on her
to charge the nights with dangerous new verse.

A former national
newspaper reporter in the UK
and South Africa,

CATO PEDDER

is now working towards her first poetry
collection alongside a work of literary
journalism. She also writes poetry reviews
for website *Write Out Loud* and recently
completed an MA in Poetry Writing.
Pedder lives and works in Bristol.

Things That Make Us Fly

That was the future: codas of grass and fever,
hollowed out, hauling the engine of grief

from room to room; songs straining at darkness
as we strain towards the liminal, the light

at the window; tomorrow running like mercury
down the spine of a broken book. Those songs

were thieves of the lifted page, or of hope:
can I make it clear? The first hint is rain

and the second, meadows: ox-eyed daisy,
sorrel, cowslip; ragged robin pinkly bleeding.

Clenched in the palm of who knows what God
we unwind in a dance of spiralling light

or Hopkins' shook foil, his faith unravelling
into a thousand trembling leaves.

CLAIRE QUIGLEY

has had poems published
in a variety of magazines, including *Magma,
Gutter, The Interpreter's House, Other Poetry,* and
Obsessed with Pipework. Her photos have
appeared on a number of book and CD covers
and in magazines and she was awarded an
Edwin Morgan Travel Bursary for a project
involving poems and photographs on the theme
of 'A Dry Atlantis – Britain and Rising Sea
Levels'. She lives in Glasgow where she works
with CoderDojo Scotland, part of a global
collaboration which provides free coding
clubs for young people.

The Botanic Lighthouse

Our marriage was an arid place, a room
of sand in which we traced out silent
patterns on the floor to brush away.

He had green fingers, slipped them on
like gloves each morning, as he left
to tend his plants under their static sky.

He'd stay with them as long as it was light,
sometimes longer, while I pressed my back
against the space left in our bed.

When the sea rose he was wild, searching
for safety. Sent me and half his garden
to this light to wait for him; he never came.

Since then I've let the plants grow as they
please, they fill the rooms, run up and down
the shell-heart spiral of the stairs.

The air is warm, inlaid with all their coloured
scents. I move among them, small as in
a childhood garden run to seed.

I sleep inside the lantern room, glass walled
its flame blown out, the roof a copper flower
stalk to the sky. Sometimes I wake

to see it bloom, lightning like water
through electric veins. Or hear the edge
of silence as the fog rubs out the moon

while I, the green night round me
skin to bliss, watch galaxies
of fireflies through the leaves.

CLARISSA AYKROYD

grew up in Victoria, Canada
and now lives in London, England.
Her work has appeared in *The Ofi Press*,
Lighthouse, *The Island Review*, *The Missing
Slate*, *Shot Glass Journal*, *And Other Poems*,
Ink Sweat & Tears and in anthologies, and
she was a contributor to Ireland's *The
Gathering Poem*. She is a Pushcart
Prize nominee.

From The Dream-Break Out Of Sleep

From the dream-break out of sleep,
with a jolt of fear or perhaps
it was delight, which nonetheless
can be shock, and with that shudder
in the body which might be revelation,
I woke up, turning and turning
on the floor like a car's lights
manoeuvring in darkness
and asking myself, asking asking
a question which is now outside memory.

COLIN DARDIS

is a poet, editor, creative writing
tutor, freelance arts facilitator and
mental health advocate. His work has
been published widely throughout Ireland,
the UK and the USA. He is the founder of
Poetry NI, a multi-media, multi-project
platform for poetry in Northern Ireland.
Colin is also the online editor
for *Lagan Press*.

Easter Tuesday, 1941

Bring in the unidentified and the lost,
the fallen, the two hundred and fifty-five,
we shall not abandon them in this hour.

In here, we're used to asking 'at what cost?'
but none should pay this much to stay alive,
all of us were caught in that fierce shower.

Relatives arrive to inspect the dead:
they hunt for their missing, last seen awake,
discard strange faces like unwanted goods.

You see the eyes scan, the shake of the head,
a purchase no one is ready to make,
then all of a sudden, their search concludes:

they're freshly laid out, all bloodied and bold,
a couple of young souls, recently sold.

Following heavy German bombing of Belfast on Easter Tuesday 1941,
St George's Market was used as an emergency mortuary. Some 700 people
were killed during the raids with 255 bodies brought to the market for
identification.

DAISY BEHAGG

won the Bridport Prize for Poetry 2013. In 2014 she won the Templar portfolio prize for her short pamphlet *Cockpit Syndrome*, and was shortlisted for the Melita Hume Poetry Prize. Her work has been published in numerous journals including *The Poetry Review, Poetry Wales, Ambit, The North, The Rialto* and *Poems in Which*, and she has read at events across the country including the Edinburgh Book Festival, London's Troubadour, Boomtown Festival and for Next Generation Poets. She lives in Brighton.

Vesperae Solennes de Confessore

I love Mozart especially
this one piece whose name is in
Latin when I looked it up it turned
out to be a piece of sacred music
which was out of character but listening
to the woman lifting her voice in the way
that is to normal speech what poetry
prayer or the wordless cries we make
at the height of grief or of lovemaking
are to normal speech you don't
really need to know what the words
mean you can tell she's
singing about something
sacred anyway

DAVID SPITTLE

has recently completed a PhD
on the poetry of John Ashbery in relation
to Surrealism at Newcastle University.
He has published reviews in *Hix Eros* and
PN Review. His poetry has been published
in *3am, Zone, The Shadowtrain,* and is translated
into French courtesy of *Black Herald Press*.
In addition to poetry, he has written the libretti
to three operas, performed at various venues
around Cardiff and at Hammersmith Studios
in London. In 2014 Spittle was commissioned
to write a song cycle for the Bergen National
Opera, which has since been performed
in venues across Manchester,
London and Bergen.

Amer

I have to run else I will be found
not that I know who she is or what she wants
just the sound, heard through doors, of teeth
turning wide their keyholes in shock

to find her

put in mind of a playground swing set
five silvered lines dropped in vertical precision
while two at either end swung in pendulous refrain
fastened to the necks of children

not that I know who she is or what she wants
just a piano drop witness caught in the doorway
turning wide their keyholes in shock
unable to look away from what she saw

as she unties

five silvered lines dropped in vertical precision
lending Newton's Cradle a geometry
fastened to the necks of children
to serenely dance a perfect arc

just a piano drop witness caught in the doorway
rushing to reconcile the doll with its house
unable to look away from what she saw
standing with her face, newly hers and facing her

her self and walks to

lending Newton's Cradle a geometry
as apples fall short of the ground, held to levitate
to serenely dance a perfect arc
in the flourish of these laws rewritten

rushing to reconcile the doll with its house
and how she had grown up into those hands
standing with her face, newly hers and facing her
gloved with his grip, the iris flooding to change

where you watch

as apples fall short of the ground, held to levitate
and in doing so they conceal her eyes, now wide open
in the flourish of these laws rewritten
to find her as she unties herself and walks to where you watch

Poetry enabled
DEBRIS STEVENSON
to decipher her dyslexia, so she now teaches
poetry as an alternative vocabulary. She's been
followed by Channel 4, toured internationally
and been published by the likes of *Magma,* Louis
Vuitton and had her debut pamphlet *Pigeon
Party* released by Flipped Eye in 2014.
Curve Associate Artist, Founder and
Artistic Director of the Mouth Poets,
Debris is currently working on a Grime
and poetry exchange project kickstarted
by a Live Lounge collaboration for
BBC 1xtra with MC
Lady Leshurr.

Dutch Pot Dancing

Hardly Belafonte, King, Black Jesus, Stokely, Malcolm X or Rap.
Bungled trophies. Their country is a nation on no map.
Gwendolyn Brooks, 'The Blackstone Rangers'

In the back of a Dutch Pot shop, 200 sweating bodies hardly
smell of anything. It's a happy stink. We're Belafonte
banana boats inventing Calypso with motions. Kings
of testosterone. We pack in until even the air is Black.
Hair new and waxed. We are happy being 16, as Jesus
might have been. Singing 'follow the leader.' Leaders, Stokely,
presidents of panther mentality, beautiful as violent Malcolm
when he was real-life-living, before the power of X.

Pelvises kissing. I haven't drunk or smoked a thing or
had time to decide if I want to. Hips learning flow like rap.
Little boys learn to hold bigger girls. Heads bungled
into pink lace front wigs, passing out plastic-cup-punch trophies,
smells of bass, tastes of steamed up windows. Synchronised. Their
feet drawing patterns like 8 year old fingers from car seats. A country
made of multi-coloured beats. Fenugreek and clove over meat is
sometimes enough for peace and a party. Enough for me to be a
dancehall queen. Enough for all of us to taste at home in a nation
where statistics can only expose a cocktail-stick. I lead the chants on
'Trinidad... follow the leader... raise ya' hand... love and unity.' No
one can shout louder. But everyone can add a new move to our map.

EDWARD DOEGAR

lives in Brixton and works at
the Poetry Society. His poetry, translations
and reviews have appeared in various magazines
including *Poetry Review*, *Poetry Ireland Review*,
Prac Crit, *Poetry London* and *Poetry Wales*. He is a
fellow of The Complete Works, a programme
promoting diversity in British poetry, and
six of his poems feature in the Bloodaxe
anthology *Ten: The New Wave*. He is
an assistant editor at *The Rialto*.

Four Love Lyrics

I

Finding a harp
In my hip
He plays me
Raising my skin
To his fingers

My breath breaks
At his touch

II

Belly down
In the fickle grass
He builds me a necklace
A fastening of daisies

I see each stalk
Undone
From the lightest tip
Of his thumbnail

I can already taste
His hand
In my mouth
Sharp and green

III

Before he wakes
I bring my hand
Back from the window
Stubborn with dew

As if each drop
Might burn
He holds his belly tight
As he wakes

IV

Was I white
Until his hands
Covered me

Until I learnt
Their dark miles

ELIZABETH PARKER

grew up in The Forest of Dean. She achieved
a First Class Honours degree in English and
Creative Writing at Warwick University and has
been published in *Magma* and *The Stony Thursday
Book*. She has been shortlisted for The Bridport
Prize and The Melita Hume Poetry Prize. She
currently lives on the harbour in Bristol and is a
member of the Bristol poetry group The Spoke.
Her pamphlet *Antinopolis* will be out in
the Aviator series from Eyewear
in 2016.

Rivers

My father's river has risen
above seams that won't be softened or stolen
from hard lime and coal
to pennant sandstone that gives
until the water is precious
Pewter

My sister's brook is root beer with rot
the dead giving up their tannins
letting riches from their skins

My grandfather's river floats rafts of flotsam
scum bobs and pops near its walls
He says it has turned from pea to tea
that his favourite part
sometimes flows the wrong way

My friend is afraid
of her river's urge for her

Despite wide-mouthed sewers
my grandmother's river still licks up storms

My mother's river keeps forking
thinning to little more than shine
Her deft eye gathers its frays
slicks them back to their source

My brother's river
broods behind loch gates

My aunt's river grazes its banks

and widens
Rocks are loosed to salt her river

Some drink from their rivers
morsels of light and water
speck their lips

My uncle's river remembers its monks
their nights rowing to secret mass
prows cutting water bonds
to rock chapels in the gorge

My river reaches for me
At night I watch my river
slink toward my feet

Stormwater has thickened my grandmother's river
sluicing darkness from the banks

My father's river has broken through
soothes dry mud
allows fish

My friend's river has dropped
can't reach its own watermark
etching of sand that flakes as it dries

This morning my river was high
green and urgent with rain
rushing light and leaves toward the estuary

I have seen it slow
ease its freight of yachts and light

thickened with dark loads

cradling neon

swilling
a dun afternoon

In summer people meet at my river
their bare legs tassel its banks

ERICA McALPINE

has had poems appear in many
magazines including *The Times Literary
Supplement*, *The Spectator*, *Slate*, *Ambit*,
The New Criterion, and *Stand*. She teaches
literature at Keble College, Oxford,
where she lives with her husband
and two children. Her first collection
of poems, *The Country Gambler*,
will appear later this year.

Corinth

If we'd sailed here on a boat, and not this bus,
perhaps you could love – *we* could love together –
so blue a bay, tucked down under rocky hills,
and those salt-white bluffs.

But the place has wounded only one of us,
leaving a live horse and a hurt horse tethered.
Just moving the same way is hard; standing still's
also proving tough.

Above us, noisy gulls fuse and disperse, fuse
and disperse, or gather, and fly in feathered
unison over worn-out earth and sea-swells
suddenly turned rough.

ERIN FORNOFF

is a Dublin resident
who has been published in *The Stinging
Fly, New Planet Cabaret, The Irish Times, Skylight
47*, and others. In 2014 she was selected for the
Poetry Ireland Introductions Series. She was
2013 winner of the StAnza Digital Slam and
won 3rd in the Strokestown International Poetry
Award, judged by Michael Schmidt. She was
highly commended in the Over the Edge New
Writer of the Year in 2012 and won the 2003
Cellar Door First Prize for Poetry. She has
performed her poetry at Glastonbury, StAnza,
Cheltenham Literature Festival, and dozens
of other events, including a national tour of
Ireland. She has received a Literature Bursary
from the Irish Arts Council and has an
MPhil with Distinction in Creative
Writing from Trinity
College Dublin.

Thigh

Thigh folded to thigh,
a rising like
strings tugged stiff
for tuning, then strummed –
thumb against a bottom lip,
breath
      like something ripping

FRANÇOISE HARVEY

grew up on the Isle of Man, but now lives in
North East England. Her poetry and short
stories have appeared in publications including
For Books' Sake's *Furies*, *Bare Fiction*, *Synaesthesia
Magazine*, *The Interpreter's House*, *Litro* and *Envoi*.
She has also been a chosen Broadsheet poet
in *Agenda*. She has a BA in Creative Writing
from the University of Wales, Bangor,
and is editorial associate and ebook
whisperer at *Mslexia* magazine.

Sewing In The Stones

She used blind stitch for a weighted hem
never meant to be seen, but still neat
deep takes of thread forced through
layers of cotton and chiffon, cheesecloth and taffeta.
She frowned at each knot and unpicking,
punching and poking chains, satins and stems,
till lilies grew, rooted in the planted stones,
in thread coloured for the sky and surface she'd disturb.

It fit. A nightgown with pockets sized for hands
full, each, of the garden gravel,
long enough to cover feet
filthy from the paths she walked,
bending to scoop quartz and unsparked flint,
shears of slate from the roof,
friendly fossil ridges suspended in tar,
a lava tear she was told could float
and one plain pebble which fit neat into her hand
like an egg.

Night water is dense: the shadows thicken it like salt,
so it was a slow sinking and the stones were comfort
as the tide unbound her, and the seeping cold woke her,
and she saw her breath float by as stars.

HOLLY CORFIELD CARR

is a poet based in Bristol where she has
worked as writer-in-residence at contemporary
art centre Spike Island and the University of
Bristol's Poetry Institute. She received an
Eric Gregory Award in 2012 and in 2014 was
Highly Commended by Faber New Poets,
developing new work with the Jerwood /
Arvon Mentoring Scheme and Clare Pollard
throughout 2015. Her pamphlet *MINE*,
documenting a series of site-specific
performances in an eighteenth-century
crystal grotto commissioned as part of
the Bristol Biennial, was published
by Spike Island in 2014. She is currently
studying for a PhD at the University
of Cambridge.

Loxodrome

1 The journey from London to Sydney during which
the pilot responds to a medical emergency by turning
around over the ocean and flying back to Dubai.

⌒

2 The journey from summer to winter during which the
plane opens its doors in the desert at midday.

⌒

3 The journey from night to dawn to dawn to dawn
during which the plane's wingtip points at the sun and
we eat dinner three times but never arrive at breakfast.

⌒

4 The journey reimagined with you as the passenger
suffering a medical emergency and me as the man in aisle
seat 51F.

⌒

5 The journey reimagined with you as the receding
breakfast.

⌒

6 The journey reimagined with me as the jettisoned fuel
and you as Sydney.

⌒

7 The journey reimagined with me as the horizon and you
as the pink yolk of dawn.

⌒

8 The journey reimagined as the time it takes my hand to move across your face.

⌢

9 The journey reimagined with the medical emergency as a hijacking and the ease with which this thought passes behind the eyes of everyone I can see through the crack between my seat and 51F as the tone of voice I would leave on your voicemail.

⌢

10 The journey reimagined as further reductions on leisure time in duty free and me bulkbuying sleep for the year ahead.

IAN M DUDLEY

has published poems in
Oxford Poetry, The Dark Horse,
The Interpreter's House, The North,
and *Wasafiri*. He was a 2014 Jerwood/
Arvon poetry mentee.

Heartbreak Tattoo

I'm in the chair, the guy
says *What can I do?*
I say mark me for life
with a heartbreak tattoo.

He asks *How's that look?*
'cause I don't know.
I say like bad luck,
or the smell of snow.

It's not in your head
so you can't forget,
it's written in ink
in every cell.

Your skin tastes of salt,
you're living on pills,
you're perfectly normal,
and permanently ill.

You'll never get well,
so it's best not to beg;
find comfort in hell,
and hope for less.

My daughter got one
now I want one too:
I can't leave her alone
with a heartbreak tattoo.

ISABEL ROGERS

is the current Hampshire Poet
Laureate 2016. Her work has been widely
published (including *Poetry Wales*, *Under the
Radar*, *Mslexia* and *Poetry*). She won the 2014
Cardiff International Poetry Competition,
has been shortlisted in various national
competitions and has collaborated
with composer Ian Stephens on choral
settings of her poems.

The Apiarist

Your heart was like the bees
my childhood remembers, visited
with the old man who wouldn't let me veil
or glove. *Let the hive know you,*
he said, smiling through his cloak
of yellow and black. I swallowed
our criminal objective.

How does one befriend a bee?
Every day fewer of them died
embedded in my flesh. I grew
accustomed to the hot pain
and swell, they to the small friend
of their friend. Soon I could reach
inside the screens to burgle,
leaving counterfeit sugar as a truce.
I fancied they even welcomed it.

In summer a new queen rose.
They swarmed, shimmering over the orchard:
an alien steering west to the low sun
and away, leaving my placebo syrup.
What I wouldn't give to be stung again.

JAMES NIXON

lives in London and has
an MA in Creative Writing from
Royal Holloway. In 2015, James was the
Emerging Writer Fellow at Cove Park and
has since had poetry published in *Ambit*. He
is currently a Voiced Writer-in-residence at
Phytology, Bethnal Green, a commission funded
by the Arts Council England and is working
on a PhD concerning hauntological
poetics.

It's 11.26 in SE13

& I am wearing too many clothes to be jack-
            knifing athletic on a chocked stock-still
Lewisham High Street.   If only it would rain
I'd feel cool   & wise that I wore this hot wax
jacket. But the sun is buoyant as a medicated mood
& I am bothered
            shouldering bodies in the market,
            sweating through slowly as a hangover.

When I left you were spreading   across
our sprung bed, light like a handkerchief
wiping down
your back made of butter. I miss that
as a punch-up in Specsavers flowers pavement-wise,
women spill out wind-milling & screaming hoodoo.

Closer to the bakery a jaundiced man
is filing his nails
on a brick wall & kids are giving colloquies
about domestic violence from a traffic island.
            All this time
you're asleep on the bed in my head
until I really come home with a dowry of croissants.

Our London, love, is a patient getting sicker, jouncing
with fever from mono Bow Church,
to saturnine Clapham South.
But when eventually I am rheumy & slow   & worse
than this place which somehow careens on
& our futuristic children ask what the city is,
snatching at my memories for some kind of quiddity,

I will have no other words but the clear
      & all of a sudden
            'It's a good place to love'.

JASON ENG HUN LEE

was born in the UK in 1984.
He has been published in the UK,
Singapore and Hong Kong, was nominated
by *Cha: An Asian Journal* for a Pushcart Prize,
and was a finalist for the Hong Kong University
Prize (2010) and runner-up for the Melita Hume
Prize (2012). He has a PhD in English Literature
and currently lectures at Hong Kong
Baptist University.

In Your Absence

I said when you moved into my life,
'fill the room and the room will be yours',
so you took possession of everything
and set them to darkness in your absence.

They will not forget your subtle grace:
the sofa stoops to pick up your weight,
the jar shows you its well of desire, even
the letters spread and fly from memory.

Would that you had not been kind to them,
that you had simply glanced at each object,
not turning your hands over each thing,
filled every cushion with a heart of feathers,

made every cord a connection, switched
the lights on from each remote location.
Tell me then this was not your parting gift,
that you had not joined with their reflections.

Now they pine for you, they clamour as I do
for your presence, your figure walking
through each door, each sudden precipice,
each numb footstep burning in the dark,

so cold to the touch, so absent in spirit.
So full of the love you invested here.
They move only to the command
of the dark shadow you leave behind.

JEN CALLEJA

is a writer, literary translator
from German, editor and musician.
Her debut poetry collection *Serious Justice* is
forthcoming with *Test Centre*. She was
shortlisted for Eyewear Publishing's Melita
Hume Poetry Prize 2015. She is acting editor
of *New Books in German*, founder and editor of
Anglo-German arts journal *Verfreundungseffekt*,
translator in residence at the Austrian Cultural
Forum London and columnist for literature
in translation for *The Quietus*. Her latest book
translation is *Nicotine* by Gregor Hens, published
by Fitzcarraldo Editions (2015).
She lives in London.

You Must Have Thought About It

Disgusting, evil, sick, monstrous, unthinkable
The louder the outrage the more likely
you've thought about it.
You've maybe not gripped the idea by both handles
not ever sipped at the cup
but in a weak moment
in solitude of bedroom, office bathroom
waiting on a park bench, parked up in the driver's seat
slow promenade around the shopping centre,
you've hungered, looking through the keyhole of a locked door
at the half-open drawer
with ribbons, strips of zips, blister packs of pearl buttons
spilling out, not even the finest, just
not for you.

JESSICA MAYHEW

's début pamphlet, *Someone Else's Photograph*, was
published by Crystal Clear Creators in 2012. She
has twice been shortlisted for the Melita Hume
Poetry Prize. She graduated from University
College London with an MA in 2013, and
then taught abroad in SouthEast Asia.
Her second pamphlet *Amok* is part
of the Eyewear 20/20 series edited
by Les Robinson.

Hiver

Just how I imagined the house as a child,
locked empty in the day
without us to map it –

I've found it. Now I push through forks,
forested and coaxing kitchen shadows
while spoons bloom like magnolias.

I feel my way upstairs,
the pine boards split
to count an age. One hundred, two.

Vines cling to the posts,
and from somewhere, a river runs
swithering bright as lightning,

floor rubbed raw to granite.
Here, the day is dim,
dusk silting low through the hallway.

The carpet is frozen into hackles,
like the nape of the wolf I half-see
sloping into the bedroom,

lips snarled into the beginnings of words,
and my breath comes cold.
Underfoot, bones of small animals snap,

then larger: a piano-keyed jawbone,
femur. Beyond where the curtains
should hang, a stag cocks one ear,

hounding, at his hooves,
a tattered crow, blood-shocked
with both wings broken.

I still remember the duvet,
laced with hoarfrost,
the winter-lake crack as I pulled it back.

Too bad, then, that everything we dream,
we dream in the dark.
I lie down, touch your arm.

KARL O'HANLON

was born in Belfast.
He was a Fulbright scholar
at Georgetown University before
moving to York. He has published in
*Stand, Agenda, Blackbox Manifold,
The Junket*, and *Tears In The Fence*.
He is co-founder of
Eborakon.

Clifford's Tower

for the Jews of York

Have we forgotten the astringent
voice of Silkin, on frigid conscience
stupefied? Its queue-badgering ghost
must shake the iron-ribbed ceiling

of Leeds train station, the student
dives, places words choose to fester
under the skin. Plates of ice barge
the Ouse; two gulls ride convections

of air, mewing like remnant heralds
of some old Norse saga. The heart
brims over. Incongruity is shorn
of terror; hobby Vikings at Costa

warm their close-braided cheeks
with the cups. *Malebisse* sounds
like morning mist, halitosis low
over the stray, the derangement

of light so that there comes easy
to the imagination some deity –
its immense hands over us –
bending light pink and green

(though whether in design loving
or unloving impossible to say).
Conscience, we might well think,
is a kind of bad debt. Shake it off.

Heap ashes on it. To conclude
this weekend's jolly, Clifford's
tower burns again. Illuminations
lave the cold stone face, sparks

streaming down gilt-golden like
hyperactive tears; and afterward,
a girning skull vomiting smoke,
lobotomised. All applaud.

What can steel in us remembrance
of the freezing blade on shoulder
-blade, fear's stone-encircled echo
and fire: its hunger, sad, satiable?

What can render love at its limits,
real sexual love, hounded by hate;
and in that northern *walpurgisnacht*,
true horror of their final non-choice?

KATHERINE SHIRLEY

has had poems appear in *Snakeskin, Poems Underwater, the New Verse News,* the Gold Dust calendar 2012 and *Soul Vomit.* Her work *The Water Way* was lock no. 87 on the Rochdale Canal Festival Poetry Trail 2012. She has been featured as a performance poet at the Ashmolean Museum, the Stockwell Festival, The Word Café in Teddington and as a guest on the Julie Mullen Mad House Radio Show. She is a native Londoner.

D Is For Denial

We don't die in Sheffield, lass
Fit as a fiddle, me
I'll pop another brew on
And get tha' gob round our Jan's chutney
We just sat there as he fussed
A picture in his sweats and tee
Of how things change from year to year
When you don't see much family
The photos came out, one by one
I cooed at grandkids' gap-toothed glee
Ignored the question how 'bout us
And dunked a biscuit in cold tea
He shuffled off to find your gift
You held the box closed on your knee
Unspoken words at grandad's watch
In Sheffield, lass, we Dee.

LIZ QUIRKE

lives in Spiddal, Co. Galway,
Ireland with her partner and daughter.
Her poetry has been published in journals and
anthologies including *Southword, Crannóg, The
Stony Thursday Book* and *The Ofi Press*. She was
shortlisted for the Cúirt New Writing
Prize in 2015 and won the 2015
Poems for Patience
Competition.

Rite

There will be a changing of the guard,
if such ceremony will be allowed,
a dusting down of dampers to
purge all lamps and lights.
Shops will mourn from their facades,
black-ribboned in the old way.
Passers-by will nod and scuttle
to spurn the mists of death.
Great coats will be sponged as they were before,
and shoes spit-shone to a pitch-like gleam.
The footfall slap will ring out around the streets.
Wedding services kept for cakes
will peek from muslin blankets
to sour-crust dry triangles,
while whiskey flows like speech.
Clocks will chime only grief notes,
humming deep into the silence.
Eyelid mirrors will reflect the dark beneath.
Running along on idle tracks,
children will be shunned
from the adult world
palming flowers in the breeze
to mimic final kisses not received.

LORNA COLLINS

is an artist, poet, writer and
arts educator. She completed her PhD as a
Foundation Scholar in French Philosophy at
Jesus College, Cambridge. Collins spent ten
years in academia, studying and teaching. In this
period she was the founder and co-organiser/
curator of the trans-disciplinary *Making Sense*
colloquia and co-editor of the series of *Making
Sense* books. She is the author of a monograph
published in 2014 with Bloomsbury, *Making
Sense: Art Practice and Transformative Therapeutics*.
She is also the co-editor of *Deleuze and the
Schizoanalysis of Visual Art*.

Altamira

The air chokes with smoky dust
I inhale a scent of biker's rust
mixed with coconut and pure heat
roasting a market of rotting meat
and rippling the horizon.

It's an arid saffron sauna
the Orient in the summer.
Here I am:
a sore, ungainly thumb
amidst the tawny, tiny natives.

I came in search of an earth
which had touched my eyes and given birth
to a new sensibility —
a sublime that could set me free,
and nourish my weary senses.

This table-eau weeped an orange nectar
my eyes plunged into its vector
gorging on its flaxen paint
which flickered light without restraint
an indulgent sponge for my senses.

The painter said he'd found his vision
infused across the Orient; a collision
of fulvid colours and healing aromas,
a sense of life where the earth shimmers
and invites you in to settle.

So I became a gypsy
following my nose, ever tipsy,

tracking the scent that sang from a painting
and touched my soul – a tainting
I craved to source in the East.

I travelled across the continent
my eyes squeezing more illuminant
from the life and love I found out there
where pollen and parasols filled the air
honouring the sunshine.

The monks would walk in their orange robes
and then sit, set apart from a capitalist globe,
to ponder the mondial orb and let go:
Sartori received from time's dropped flow
where all people are your brethren.

The children held my heart
when they clasped my hand, in the wat
where we would pray together,
reaching further into this tether
of living peace.

They would call me sister
and give me rice and water.
We drew the world together
I soaked up colour from tropical weather
and painted my own sublime.

MARIA ISAKOVA-BENNETT

lives in Liverpool where she works
as a poet and artist for charities, reads and runs
workshops in art galleries, and is collaborating
with artists and writers in the UK, Ireland and
UAE. She has an MA in Creative Writing from
Lancaster University. She has poetry and reviews
in print and online in the UK, Ireland and the
US. Her poetry has been placed, shortlisted,
and highly commended in several international
poetry competitions, and she was awarded
first prize in Ver Poets Open Competition with
her poem 'Adrift'. Her first pamphlet,
Caveat, is published by Poetry
Bus Press in Ireland.

Adrift

It's November and half way through the Our Father
when Richie lifts his head and slurs 'Halloween

be thy name.' We serve plates of food –
little rescue rafts on an uncertain sea.

Even the homeless centre reminds me of you:
the way you talked to the man on the street in Dublin,

bought him a meal in The Bleeding Horse and told him
you'd just lost God. I didn't know who was helping who.

Richie shovels bolognese, his head hits the table.
Coaxed into standing, he slides

backwards and forwards in unlaced shoes,
'Come on lad! Come on mate!'

A bruise for a face. He falls and rises, slips
and staggers away between unsteady men.

The chairs are wiped, the floor is brushed,
we wash our hands, and the room steadies.

I remember O'Shea on the steps of The Merrion Hotel –
clean-shaven, his hand out for money, his soft voice.

I gave him five euros just to listen to his story
and wondered if he knew you:

the Good Samaritan from Fermanagh
clutching *National Geographic* shouting

'There is nothing. Only this.'

MATT HOWARD

lives in Norwich,
where he works for the RSPB.
He is also a steering group member of
New Networks for Nature, an eco-organisation
that asserts the central importance of landscape
and nature in our cultural life. His debut
pamphlet, *The Organ Box*, was
published by Eyewear in
December 2014.

Making Evelyn's Tables

Omnia explorate; meliora retinete

It begins with a crime, a man dead,
outside of God. Then the felling of an evergreen,
a pine, from this they will make planks,
with tongue and groove to bind them, glued
with animal collagen from skin, tendon, hooves.
Last, a varnish: honey, cedar or poppy oil.

The man will be pinned in preparation,
his veins, nerves, arteries, set in a triptych.
He will display like a winter birch, each branch
bare of fruit, the crown wracked.
In the absence of viscera he will abstract
to the spaces between bone and flesh.

Then we will truly behold a man
for ourselves; trace the inner workings,
the circuit that oxygenates blood;
the sympathetic system of fight or flight,
endings that cause sweats, the heart to race,
stripped into lines of his feeling.

MATTHEW PAUL

was born in New Malden in 1966
and still lives, and works, on the outskirts of
London. He was shortlisted for the Poetry
School/Pighog Press pamphlet prize in 2013 and
has had poems published in a variety of places,
including *Magma*, *Poetry Ireland Review* and *The
Rialto*. He co-edits *Presence* haiku journal,
co-edited/wrote *Wing Beats: British Birds in
Haiku* (Snapshot Press, 2008) and is an
occasional contributor to the *Guardian*'s
'Country Diary' column.

The Skip

In no time after arrival that morning
at number nine, it was full to overflowing
with everyone else's shite, from all along

Tennyson Terrace. I'd itched to stay up late,
until well past my bedtime, to watch folk nip out
by moonlight and deposit the usual tat:

mattresses stained with a Turin shroud of spunk;
an analogue telly that would break a man's back
if he lugged it on his own; three-legged chairs, Coke

cans, clotted condoms; miscellaneous crap.
But what no-one expected underneath the heap,
when at last they carted it off to the tip,

was a head- and limb-less Caucasian man,
whose identity the Police would never learn,
in bloat stage; a gutful of maggoty churn.

I curse like a barrow boy for missing my turn.

MATTHEW STEWART

was born in Farnham, Surrey, in 1973.
Following a comprehensive school education, he
took a degree in Modern Languages at St Peter's
College, Oxford. For the last eighteen years he
has lived between West Sussex and Extremadura,
Spain, where he works as the export manager
and blender for a local winery. He has published
two pamphlets with HappenStance Press
(*Inventing Truth*, 2011 and *Tasting Notes*, 2012).
His poems have also been widely
published in UK magazines such
as *Ambit, London Magazine*
and *The Rialto*.

Boiling Point

Until you've lived in a country
full of kitchens full of saucepans
that slowly creak to the boil,
a kettle won't seem to whistle
like the owner of a loose dog
calling it back, calling it home.

MICHAEL NAGHTEN SHANKS

is the editor of online literary journal
The Bohemyth. His own writing is featured in
various publications, including *Gorse, Poetry
Ireland Review, 3:AM Magazine* and *The Quietus*.
In 2015 he was shortlisted for the Melita Hume
Poetry Prize and was selected to read as part of
the Poetry Ireland Introductions Series. He has
read his work at numerous events, including
at the New Writers' Salon during Listowel
Writers' Week, as part of the Young Irish
Writers' Showcase in the London Irish Centre,
on RTÉ Radio 1 and during the International
Literature Festival Dublin. His debut poetry
pamphlet, *Year of the Ingénue*, is available
from Eyewear Publishing.

Ingénue (pt. 3 Parisian Hotel Interview)

Imogen White is an unusual star.   Her allure has given her time
to develop   as an actress. Now 29, she's still most known
for a single role,   playing Tom Cruise's girlfriend,
and famously shuns the limelight.   And yet there is something
about her breakthrough character,   the wide-eyed, gamine do-gooder,
that continues to define her.   A character actress trapped
in an ingénue's body, Imogen   is determined to leave
the girlfriend parts   behind: *I think that as I get older, I'm looking*
at roles that move away from that mould   and are more based
on women that are experienced   and have had a life
before the stage you find them in.   Giving up the cutesy,
doe-eyed ingénue show   was a smart move; its appeal
was wearing thin for those keen   observers who were well aware
that she was in   on the industry's secret handshake.
The extraordinary thing about her   is that whatever she's wearing –
today, it's an ivory and liquorice jumpsuit   that accentuates her tiny frame –
you can't help but focus   on her eyes, which really are as black
and as hypnotic as on screen.   Imogen White is not
simply another actress, but rather, one   who is learning to succeed
by perfecting the art   of playing herself.

NIALL BOURKE

is originally from Kilkenny in Ireland
but currently lives in London where he
teaches English Literature at St Michael's
College in Bermondsey. In 2015 he finished
an MA in Creative Writing and Teaching
at Goldsmiths. He writes both poetry and
prose and has been published in a number
of journals and magazines in the UK and
Ireland including *The Galway Review, The Irish
Literary Times, Southbank Poetry, The Bogman's
Cannon, Prole, Holdfast Magazine, Ink Sweat and
Tears* and *Roadside Fiction.* He has been longlisted
for The Short Story competition and shortlisted
for the 2015 Over The Edge New Writer Of
The Year Award (for both poetry and
fiction), The Bare Fiction Poetry Prize
and The Costa Short
Story Award.

Unexpected item in the bagging area

you say and then blink at me and I try to fathom the depths
of its unexpectedness. It is as if I have carried you

in a submarine to an underwater lecture on Egyptology
and a middle-age octopus, in a plum coloured blouse,

has just tentacled to a slide of Tutankhamun, making you
realise (for the first time and at the age of twenty-seven)

that the word sarcophagus is not pronounced sarko – FAYgus
after all. I mean, if it were a rift in the space-time continuum

or some caged animal's sandpapering of nostalgia or, even,
a hitherto prudish lover shattering unannounced the last taboo

with a kumquat, well, then I could understand. But it is a bottle
      of Prosecco.
A green one, in a supermarket. With a wine section.

PIERRE RINGWALD

holds Canadian and British passports.
He is co-founder of the *Step Up* slam poetry
night which was based in Ottawa, Canada.
Ringwald was an active performance poet in
the UK from 2001-2011. Pierre currently teaches
English and Drama at a secondary school in
Helsinki, Finland where he also co-hosts
Lauantaijatsit (Saturday Jazz) on Basso radio. His
debut pamphlet from Tall-Lighthouse, *A World
of Sudden Claws*, was the Poetry Book Society
Pamphlet Choice, Summer 2006.

Not For Silver

One

The bottle caps and tabs
littering the front porch
they were not missed.

Two

A pie plate scarecrowing
in the vegetable patch
a nuisance I blamed on the wind.

Three

A ring left on the patio table
gathered up in a sweep of wings
         I cursed my carelessness.

Four

A jangle of house keys
snatched from a lock
       I swore, double-bolting the front door.

Five

I dream of magpies
beaks bored of silver
now lusting for gold
chase glittering secrets
that shouldn't be told.

RICHARD SCOTT

was born in London in 1981.
His poems have appeared widely in
magazines including *Poetry Review*, *Poetry London*
and *Butt Magazine*. He has been a winner of
the Wasafiri New Writing Prize, a Jerwood/
Arvon Poetry Mentee and a member of
the Aldeburgh 8. He teaches poetry at the
University of Hertfordshire and talks about
opera and libretti on Resonance FM.
His pamphlet *Wound* is from
Rialto (2016).

Public Toilets In Regent's Park

The men here are bird-footed
feathering past the attendant's two-way mirror
unperturbed by the colonising micro-organisms –
bulleidia   *cobetia*   *shigellosis*

sliming across the yellowed groutings,
the fist-deep pool of brackish water
quivering in the U-bend, the tile that reads
for information on venereal disease telephone 01…

All for the thrill of placing their knees
on the piss stained cold, the iris shimmering
behind a hand-carved glory hole,
a beautiful cock unfolding like a swan's neck
from the Harris Tweed of a city gent's suit.

Whispers, gasps of contact echo
inside each nested cubicle! But careful –
the prying attendant will rattle
her bucket and mop if she spies four shoes!
Our men disperse as mallards from the face of a pond.

RISHI DASTIDAR

is a member of Malika's Poetry Kitchen.
A runner-up in the 2011 Cardiff International
Poetry Competition, and the 2014 Troubadour
International Poetry Competition, his work
has featured in the 2012 anthologies *Adventures
in Form* (Penned in the Margins) and *Lung
Jazz* (Cinnamon Press / Eyewear Publishing),
and most recently in 2014's *Ten: The New
Wave* (Bloodaxe). He also was an assistant
editor at *The Rialto* in 2015.

Thrown a loop

by life, by love? Make no grand claims
about what to do next, what can be done –
or think that you're the only one.
Grief can be borne, the past can be gone
with a simple kindness, a kiss or two.
Remember life is mostly amazing
awesome with all the capital As.
This place now, this bloom of luck
a blessing – the trick is to invent
a tradition, embrace elegance,
believe you can be better,
that the best is coming.

That the best is coming,
believe you can be better,
a tradition. Embrace elegance,
a blessing – the trick is to invent
this place now, this bloom of luck,
awesome with all the capital As.
Remember life is mostly amazing,
with a simple kindness, a kiss or two.
Grief can be borne, the past can be gone.
Think that you're the only one?
About what to do next, what can be done?
By life, by love? Make no grand claims.

ROISIN KELLY

was born in Northern Ireland and
raised in Co. Leitrim, and has since found her
way to Cork City via a year on a Mayo island.
Her poems have appeared in *The Stinging Fly,*
The Timberline Review, Southword, HARK, the
Interpreter's House, the *Aesthetica Creative Writing*
Annual 2014, and *Poetry* magazine's Young Irish
Poets issue. More of her work is forthcoming in
the *Irish Literary Review* and *The Penny Dreadful.*
Kelly has been a finalist in poetry competitions
run by *Synaesthesia* magazine, Dromineer
Literary Festival and the Red Line Book
Festival; and she won *Tethered*
by Letters' 2015 contest.

Hades

And that, for me, was love.
Sitting by your side
outside a café
on hard metal chairs

wind beginning to speak
of winter
and breathing
on our coffees' hot foam.

In summer
it was lying by the river
where it churns blackly
to the sea.

The hem of my dress lifted
just enough to tease you.
Knowing
that warmth would soon

be a memory only
as would the creak
of cider cans
the cries of gulls

and that city, we would not
live there forever
even then
we were saying goodbye.

But you were uneasy
by the river

disturbed by my dreamings
and distant gaze

my fingers gently
brushing my own skin —
not yours —
by moments

when I might
have forgotten you.
You wanted love
to be a masterpiece

a feast.
You expected my
worshipful gaze
as you fed to me seeds

from the pomegranate
ran a bath, lit candles
wrapped me
in a white robe

led me through the steam
closed your eyes
and asked me
to kneel before you.

SAMANTHA WALTON

has published five pamphlets —
Strange House (Sadpress, 2015), *Amaranth,*
Unstitched (Punch Press, 2013), *City Break Weekend*
Songs (Critical Documents, 2011), *tristanundisolde*
(Arthur Shilling Press, 2009) and *Animal Pomes*
(Crater Press, 2015). She was Poet-in-Residence
at SoundEye Poetry Festival, Cork in 2015 and
also at the ESRC Genomics Forum in 2013. She
has read at the UEA, Surrey and Alloa poetry
festivals, and in 2013 organised the digital poetry
night Syndicate in Edinburgh. Her poems have
been published in the *Cambridge Literary Review,*
Blackbox Manifold, Be the First to Like This: New
Scottish Poetry Anthology
and *The Herald.*

Tsk Lady

In a room that seemed always to be twilight
feebly trying to wrap you up, my
light sleep broken by trains passing
each audible load; razors, gusts, shore lines, sea roar
turns us into a sound hole, a bed whose width
can't extend to embrace your absence
If two people like us trying very hard to be
lovers & nothing else can't be happy, who else?
& now I see that happiness is frugal
doesn't demand a sea change, won't be
swallowed by the churlish nostalgia of a mug
but may perch on rim or sill, and that your hands
may knot disordered constants, make pace, smooth and
        cleave contours
make shadows less jarring but less distinct
all great, all fire and, where necessary, all ablaze

SAMUEL TONGUE

has published poems in numerous
anthologies and magazines, including *And
Other Poems, Cordite, Gutter, Ink, Sweat & Tears,
Magma,* and *Northwords Now*. He held the Callan
Gordon Award as part of the 2013 Scottish
Book Trust's *New Writers Awards* and is featured
in *Be The First to Like This: New Scottish Poetry*
(Vagabond Voices, 2014). He is poetry editor
at *The Glasgow Review of Books* and lectures
in Religion, Literature, and Culture at the
University of Glasgow.

St. Thomas Aquinas a.k.a. The Jazzman

'The soul is not simply clothed with a body, nor imprisoned in a
body... it is what makes the body a living body of the kind it is,
rather as the shape of a key is what makes it the key of a particular
door, or the pitch of a note is what makes it the particular note it is.'
Aquinas, Anthony Kenny

Quiet! Aquinas, the great dumb ox,
is about to bellow, to blow wild
as a spirit in this sweating heat.
He wouldn't like it, but I think he's a jazzman –
I know, I know, you think he's way too slow,
no Theolonius Monk, more a Dominican friar –
but he's a jazzman who can blow the kind of notes
that shine, that shimmer like the gilt explosion
of saxophone in the mirrorball lights
of his shaven head and create a dancing
theatre of souls, souls that are not clothed
in a doomed prison-house of flesh, or maimed
in its damned tight straitjacket, but souls
that are sounded into being bodies,
a rolling breath running note after note
that can't be anything else but soul,
immaterial material, dancing us across
the floor, angels on pinheads of light.

STEWART CARSWELL

is from the Forest of Dean.
He currently lives in Cambridge,
working as a technical writer at a
software company. His poems
have been published by *Envoi,
Cadaverine,* and *Brittle Star*.

Shapiro's

I saw your name sunlit above the shop doorway
and so naturally I thought about you
making a living here behind the counter,
stocking and serving portions of broccoli,

although I reasoned it could not be your store
and that the name was actually someone else
calling out for you, wanting you to walk in
and talk about more than the weather.

TESS JOLLY

lives on the South Coast with
her family. She works as a library assistant
and facilitates Creative Writing workshops for
children and young people. She has a degree
in English Literature from the University of
Roehampton and a Masters Degree in Creative
and Critical Writing from the University of
Sussex. Her work has appeared in many UK
poetry magazines. Jolly has been commended
in the Four Counties Poetry Competition, the
Stanza Poetry Competition, the Barnet Arts
Poetry Competition and twice in the Mslexia
Women's Poetry Competition. Last year she was
awarded joint second place in the Stanza Poetry
Competition run by The Poetry Society and
was the winner of the Hamish Canham
Prize for her poem 'Goldfields'. Jolly's
debut pamphlet will be out in the Aviator
series from Eyewear in 2016.

Goldfields

When our children ask how we met, I'll tell them
about the fork in the river, where a carpenter called James
found flakes of gold. I'll tell them this all happened
long ago, before Great-grandmother was born,
and how the story passed from mouth to mouth
to bind a seam around the earth. I'll bring them
the shopkeeper striding through Californian streets,
holding a bottle of gilded dust before astonished eyes.
I'll compare that bottle to a spinning wheel, an egg, a harp,
the way a child might open the door to a room
she didn't know was there, reach beyond a wardrobe's fur
and feel frost lapping her fingers. I'll tell them
men travelled for months inspired by what they'd heard,
that there was violence, sickness, death – but hope
kept them moving. I'll show them the valley where some
found what they were looking for gleaming on grassy outcrops,
others waded knee-deep sifting muddied water,
and many found nothing at all. I'll explain what words
like prospect mean, and fever. I'll say that in the end
it wasn't skill or hard work or guessing the right name,
but luck that shone in those men's grateful palms, as they stood
amidst the rocks and gravel, the glistening streams.

TIFFANY ANNE TONDUT

is a writer, editor
and poetry tutor. Her work has appeared
in *The Rialto, Magma, Poetry News* and
Lung Jazz: Young British Poets for Oxfam.
She was an additional winner in the
Troubadour International Poetry
Prize 2015. She currently
resides in London.

Canary Girls

i.m 'The Canary Girls' of Munition Factories 1914–1918

No machine had ever felt the plumage of a girl.
No girl had ever flown inside the cabin of a crane
and worked it.

News broke swift – fields of houses emptied.
Whole factories beating deft with women's wings.

Every flock had tools to ply:
some hammered, quick as beaks; others preened steel
or weighed and measured, nursing bombs
with a mother's eye.

New girls hatched in night shifts –
faces bright as yolk from packing shells with TNT.

Feathers erupted – streaks of fire through skin.
Some girls burned, blew away.

V.A. SOLA SMITH

lives in Lancaster where
she works as a freelance copywriter.
She completed a Contemporary Prose
Fiction MA at Kingston University,
graduating with Distinction in 2010. She has
had flash fiction featured in Little Episodes'
anthology *Brainstorms* and her poems have been
published in *Lung Jazz: Young British Poets for
Oxfam* and *Sculpted: an Anthology of the North
West*. Her debut poetry pamphlet,
Almost Kid was published in 2015
as part of Eyewear Publishing's
20/20 series.

Exit Fee

Pig cars sponge the puddle like a trough. At their feet,
the cool palm that rubbed your face in the smut of another day's
ashes, smudging the circus costume of this city's flesh. Now
just a memory; the glimmer of a coin, hollow as a ring.
Red men shoot their flash lights. Stop! U-turn.

Expressions of no entry, converge, give way,
where disused train tracks like leather belt scars
cross out via a fresh slash of railings. Unfamiliar
faces break out like disease, rain closing in on the cobbles,
brown teeth, edged in blood. Her old corner smirks

the ironic grin of a skull prized from a girl
you were just trying to show a little love.

VICTORIA KENNEFICK

is a native of Shanagarry, Co Cork.
A Fulbright scholar, she completed her PhD
in English at University College Cork in 2009.
Her début pamphlet, *White Whale*, won the
Munster Literature Fool for Poetry Chapbook
Competition 2014 and the Saboteur Award for
Best Poetry Pamphlet 2015. She won the Red
Line Book Festival Poetry Prize 2013 and her
work has been shortlisted for many other prizes.
Poems have appeared in *Poetry, The Irish Times,
The Stinging Fly, The Penny Dreadful, The Irish
Examiner, Bare Fiction, And Other Poems,
Numéro Cinq, Banshee*, and elsewhere.
Two poems were winners of the
Hennessy New Irish Writing
Award for March 2015.

Visiting Sylvia

I find you (it's not a competition) sprouting tulips, a jar of pens.
I lay three daffodils; my new husband kneels to take a photograph.
We debate the portent of honeymoon snaps of dead poets' graves.

In the picture the wind messes with my hair, light makes me squint.
On-screen I am already in the past. I apologise to your neighbour,
step on his plot to get closer. My husband wisely wanders off.

I talk aloud, resist the weird urge to lie on top of you,
as if we'd share something else but soil. I don't think we'd have gotten on.
I tell you about my wedding, the poems I write on train tickets, on receipts,

this poem. I do cry, relieved where you're buried is wild and fierce,
that there are red tulips licking your name in metal and stone, hungry.
My husband returns with a tissue, waves it like a white flag.

Originally
from the UK,
WES LEE
currently lives in Wellington,
New Zealand. Her chapbook of short
fiction, *Cowboy Genes,* was published by Grist
Books at the University of Huddersfield and
launched at the Huddersfield Literature Festival
in 2014. She was the 2010 recipient of The
BNZ Katherine Mansfield Literary Award, and
has won a number of awards for her writing,
including The Over the Edge New Writer of
the Year Award in Ireland, and The Bronwyn
Tate Memorial Award in New Zealand. Most
recently she was selected as a finalist in The
London Magazine's Poetry Competition 2015
and the Troubadour Poetry Prize 2014; and
shortlisted for The 2014 Cork Literary Review
Poetry Manuscript Prize in Ireland.
Her poetry has recently appeared
in *Westerly, Meniscus, Poetry London,
Magma, Riptide, Cordite,*
and *NOON.*

Gilda

Her nylons – their *shush shush*
that slippery dress, that made men ridiculous.

She carried cloves in her purse to attract lovers;
and seashells, a Romany tradition to bring luck.

She liked to lift her skirt: her obvious delight in using it
as punctuation.

A pale blue duster coat, swinging around her as she walked
out into the night.

Appearing in his life like a comet
every so many years.

Notes and acknowledgements

A few of the poems selected in this anthology have previously appeared in magazines, or journals or pamphlets/chapbooks. Eyewear wishes to express grateful appreciation here to all the editors and publishers who have encouraged and supported the poets in this book, especially for permitting reprinting here.

'Georgia On My Mind' was first published in *The Quietus*.

'Goatscape Monologue' was first published in *Rouge States* (Oystercatcher, 2014).

'Boiling Point' was first published in *Ambit*.

'St. Thomas Aquinas a.k.a. The Jazzman' was first published in *Spellwinders: The Clydebuilt Jazz Ensemble*. Ed. Jim Carruth. (Dreadful Night Press, 2011).

'Visiting Sylvia' was first published in *Bare Fiction Magazine* Issue 5.

'Public Toilets in Regent's Park' was previously published in *Poetry Review* and appears in *Wound* (Rialto, 2016).

'Amer' originally appeared in *The Black Herald #5*.

'Shapiro's' was first published in *Brittle Star Issue 35*.

'Goldfields' was first printed in *Poetry News*.

TODD SWIFT

was born in 1966 in Montreal,
Canada but is now also British. He is the
Director of Eyewear Publishing. Holding a PhD
from the UEA, he has had nine full poetry collections
of his work published in America, Canada, Great Britain
and Ireland. His tenth, out in his 50th year, is
Madness and Love in Maida Vale. His poems
have appeared for over 30 years in many
international publications, including *Blackbox
Manifold, The Globe and Mail, Poetry,
Poetry Review, Poetry London, The Guardian,
The Daily Telegraph, Prism International,
The Fiddlehead, Matrix* and *The Moth.*
Recently, a poem of his was
selected for *Best British
Poetry 2014.*

KELLY DAVIO

is the poetry editor and
co-publisher of *Tahoma Literary Review*,
the Senior Poetry Editor of Eyewear Publishing, and
the former Managing Editor of *The Los Angeles Review*.
She is the author of the poetry collection *Burn This
House* (Red Hen Press, 2013). A multiple Pushcart
nominee, Davio has published poems in journals
including *Best New Poets*, *The Cincinnati Review*, *Gargoyle*,
Poetry Northwest, and others, and her nonfiction regularly
appears in venues like *The Toast*, *The Rumpus*,
The Nervous Breakdown, and *Women's Review
of Books*. She writes the column
'The Waiting Room' for
Change Seven Magazine.

EYEWEAR PUBLISHING